HERCULANEUM
RECONSTRUCTED

W9-ASK-925

PATENTED SYSTEM

HISTORICAL BACKGROUND

A s its name clearly reveals, Herculaneum's origins are associated with the mythical figure of the demigod Hercules. Recent historical research has led scholars to attribute an Etruscan origin to Herculaneum, just as with Pompeii. Subsequent events in the two ancient cities were, generally speaking, parallel, up until the conclusion of the war and occupation by the Roman army under Silla, between 89 and 80 BC.

Before Imperial occupation, the town had to be equipped with major defence systems. Many parts of these walls and ramparts are still visible today, encompassed by the homes built over the passage of time. When Imperial Rome consolidated its power in the area, Herculaneum (much like Pompeii) became a popular residential area thanks in part to the splendid climate and privileged panoramic location in the Gulf of Naples.

Both underwent a phase of significant reconstruction under Augustus; they suffered serious damage from the earthquake in 62 AD; and they were wiped out by the eruption of 79 AD that struck the two cities in different ways but with equal devastation.

Whereas the relatively thin and insubstantial stratum of eruptive material that covered Pompeii ensured that its ruins would be free of any future construction, Herculaneum was covered by a layer of hard tuff stone. The city of Resina was later built on top of the hard stone crust and in 1969 the city was renamed Ercolano.

House of the Opus Craticium.

THE ERUPTION OF 79 AD

In late August of 79 AD, Mt. Vesuvius reawakened for three terrible days in one of its most destructive moments of activity destroying three major coastal communities in the Campania region - Herculaneum, Pompeii and Stabia. Each of the towns suffered a different end due to its location with respect to the volcano. Located on the western slopes of Mt. Vesuvius, Herculaneum was first enveloped by a burning cloud (400° Celsius) and then it was covered by a river of boiling mud.

There was no way out for the inhabitants who had still not decided to escape. The mud cooled to form a solid mass of tuff stone between 16 - 25 metres thick and very difficult to remove, unlike Pompeii, which was covered by just 6 meters of ash and cinder.

Cardo IV inferior.

THE EXCAVATIONS

Aﬀter the eruption of Mt. Vesuvius in 79 AD, the homes had completely disappeared, the topography of the land was radically different and Herculaneum remained nothing more than a name for many centuries. It was not until the start of the 18th century that the first archaeological excavations took place quite by accident and the new story of Herculaneum began. A number of ancient relics were discovered in 1709 during the restoration of a villa owned by Austrian Prince and General d'Elboeuf (the Kingdom of Naples was under Austrian control at the time). An enthusiastic collector, Prince d'Elboeuf excavated the site further and found works of inestimable value that belonged to the theatre of ancient Herculaneum.

As part of a forward-thinking strategy to emphasize the importance of the archaeological treasures in the Campania region, King Charles of Naples ordered excavation works that lasted from 1738 until 1766. The hardness of the enormous volcanic mass formed by the solidification of the molten rock and lava that had covered and buried Herculaneum made excavation a very difficult undertaking. That led to the development of a "tunnel excavation" system that used methods similar to mining techniques. Exploration of the villas surrounding the Forum, the homes along the Cardo III road and Villa of the Papyri turned up works of incredible quality that were collected together in a Museum at the Royal Palace of Portici. However, the difficulty of the excavation brought the works to a standstill: it was not until 1828 that the works picked back up with open-air digs such as those in Pompeii and the tunnel system was definitively eliminated.

Pseudo Seneca, first century BC.

View of the excavations in Herculaneum with Mt. Vesuvius in the background.

The palestra.

Throughout the 19th century, the excavation was interrupted and delayed until almost it was almost abandoned in 1875 due in part to opposition by local landowners.

In 1927, almost a century from the first restart, works picked back up with a dynamic impulse driven by the untiring work of Amedeo Maiuri and later by Alfonso De Franciscis. The excavations began to proceed with vigour according to modern scientific criteria - finally marking the conquest of the true form of ancient Herculaneum.

Finally, a new season of excavations carried out with greater care began in the last part of the twentieth century. New unexpected and important discoveries were made in the seafront areas particularly. The excavations carried out during the 1980s allowed for writing a new page in history about the last days of Herculaneum. All the prior archaeological excavations had only brought to light around ten human remains. This gave rise to the common opinion that most of the population (estimated at 4500) had escaped. However, during the excavations in 1982 at a "fornix" (boathouse) on the ancient beach, 270 human bodies were found.

Bronze statue of a drunken Satyr.

THE EXCAVATED AREAS AND THE URBAN DESIGN

A large viaduct leads from the current level of the land to the level of the ancient city winding down a broad curve to the right and up to a small plaza, which faces the fronts of the buildings on the southern side of the city. The suburban district is located below at the foot of the walls.

From here, the excavated areas in ancient Herculaneum are entirely visible. It almost looks like it was mounted inside a frame formed by the still unexplored mass of tuff stone with the unmistakeable profile of Mt. Vesuvius as a backdrop. Though the volcano is responsible for destroying the city, it is also responsible for its unique survival. The regular grid design of the roads appears immediately. It is similar to the layout of most cities of the Imperial era and it quite reminiscent of a design for a military encampment. Three roads slope down towards the coast (from the left to the right they are respectively named *Cardini III, IV* and *V*: Cardini II and I are still buried below the tuff stone above the excavated area on the viewer's left).

Two roads intersect with the Cardini roads at right angles. These roads are referred to as the Decumanus roads: above we see the **Decumanus Maximus**, which was the city's main street with what is believed to be the town's Forum located between *Cardini III* and *IV*. The *Decumanus Inferior* crosses the centre of the excavated area, and the Decumanus Superior has still not been excavated.

Beautiful panoramic terraces of some of the most attractive homes in Herculaneum

6

The Fountain of Hercules. (above).
Decumanus Maximus (below).

(House of the Mosaic Atrium, House of the Deer) can be seen in front of the plaza where we stopped (at the end, above the southern perimeter wall). The remains of suburban buildings can be seen below at sea level and there are still fascinating excavations taking place there, but the work is extremely difficult due to the marshy ground.

A hint: Roads that intersect at right angles surround each city block (or *insulae*), which is marked with roman numerals. Each insulae contains several buildings and each entrance is marked with a number in arabic numerals. We will use this same classification to refer to each of the sites we visit.

Human skeletons.
The Sacred Area (on the left). Terrace of
M. Nonio Balbo (on the right).

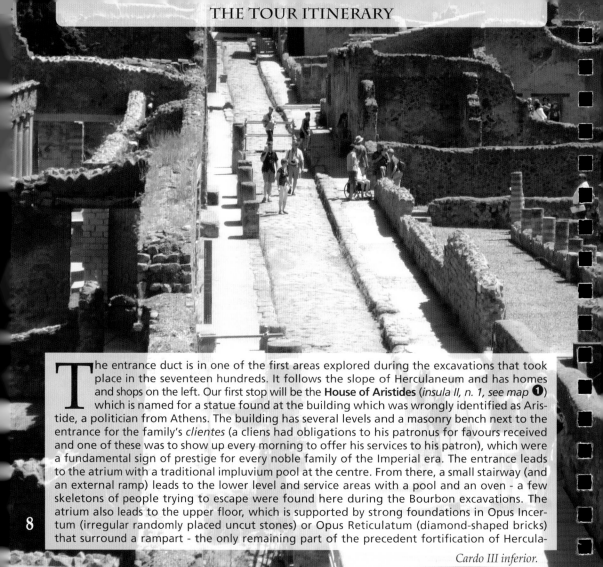

The entrance duct is in one of the first areas explored during the excavations that took place in the seventeen hundreds. It follows the slope of Herculaneum and has homes and shops on the left. Our first stop will be the **House of Aristides** (*insula II, n. 1, see map* ❶) which is named for a statue found at the building which was wrongly identified as Aristide, a politician from Athens. The building has several levels and a masonry bench next to the entrance for the family's *clientes* (a cliens had obligations to his patronus for favours received and one of these was to show up every morning to offer his services to his patron), which were a fundamental sign of prestige for every noble family of the Imperial era. The entrance leads to the atrium with a traditional impluvium pool at the centre. From there, a small stairway (and an external ramp) leads to the lower level and service areas with a pool and an oven - a few skeletons of people trying to escape were found here during the Bourbon excavations. The atrium also leads to the upper floor, which is supported by strong foundations in Opus Incertum (irregular randomly placed uncut stones) or Opus Reticulatum (diamond-shaped bricks) that surround a rampart - the only remaining part of the precedent fortification of Hercula-

8

Cardo III inferior.

neum. A tunnel from the Bourbon era connects this first home to the adjacent **House of Argus** (*insula II, n. 2, see map* ❷). This house was named for a fresco, which has now disappeared, that used to decorate a reception room, which opened onto the *peristyle* (courtyard). The overall size of the *courtyard* and the large Triclinium (formal dining room) show that the home's owners lived a healthy life with open air spaces to take the best advantage of the climate and natural resources of the zone. In front of this block of homes and shops, on the opposite side of the road, we find the secondary entrance (*insula III, n. 19, see map* ❸) to a unique site – the **House of the Inn**. The main entrance is on Cardo IV, which is parallel to the road we are on. Given its original layout and size (it is one of the largest homes on the southern side of the city) the house was mistakenly believed to have been an inn, and that is the name we still use for it today. In truth, the unique design of the house is almost entirely due to radical restoration works that were underway when the eruption took place. These are particularly evident in the north wing, which was transformed into a small independent apartment, and in one of the portico rooms, used as a shop. *(continues on page 14)*

9

House of Argus.

THE PALESTRA AND PORTICO (See guide page 15; map **8**)

The Palestra and portico face south and are surrounded on three sides by stuccoed brick columns. The portico was decorated in Pompeian fourth style paintings but only a few traces remain. The bath area was most likely the area where the better part of "social life" took place, where the people spent a large part of their day dedicated to physical health and wellness as well as human and social interaction.

The baths were a place to talk over the day, about business or even to search for favours or political support since they were the most important area where various layers of Roman Imperial society came together.

The Palestra and Portico, as it was and as it is. ➤

This house, like all those that face the southern side of the city, has a view of the sea (which was not so far then), a large panoramic terrace and a lovely portico garden (*Peristilium*). The **House of the Skeleton** (*insula III, n. 3, see map* ❹) is also located on Cardo III. Named for a human skeleton found in one of the upper floor rooms in 1831, it was one of the rare discoveries of human remains in residential Herculaneum.

This gave rise to an original hypothesis that a large part of the townspeople were able to escape in time (unlike Pompeii). The 1982 excavations mentioned earlier, which were carried out near the sea, disproved this theory.

House of the Inn (above).

This construction attracts our attention due to certain special architectural characteristics: the *atrium* is entirely covered and it has no impluvium (a pool used to collect rainwater).

Further ahead on the left we find the **House of the Genius** (*insula II, n. 3, see map* ❺), which was named for the statue of a winged cupid that crowned a marble candelabra found here. The lovely garden contained a rectangular *pool* with the short apsidal sides decorated with rich sculptured decorations as can be seen by the two marble steles at the edge of the pool. Beyond the peristyle, only a few rooms located next to the entrance were excavated back in 1828. Most of the house is still underground waiting to be rediscovered.

House of the Skeleton, central niche.

Caldarium at the Men's Baths.

In the northeast corner of this block is the *Thermopolium*, which sold food and drinks (*insula II, n. 7, see map* ❻).

Now we will cross the Decumanus Inferior and continue down Cardo III towards the Decumanus Maximus. Here, at *n. 1 (see the map* ❼) is the men's entrance to the **Central Baths**, which, as in every Roman city, were among the most important public buildings. More than just a place to bathe and practice sports, they were also social venues.

From the entrance of the *men's baths* after passing though a narrow hall, one enters into the portico of the **Palestra** whose main entrance is on Cardo IV *number 7 (see the map* ❽ *and information on page 10*). From the Palestra one re-enters the building through a large *apodyterium* (dressing room) which is well conserved with seats on the three walls and shelves above them with special compartments to hold the customers' clothing. There is also a pool in the room as well as an elegant *labrum* (a type of sink) framed by an apse on the back wall which was probably used for washing the hands and feet before entering the pool. Through a small room, one enters the *frigidarium* dedicated to cold-water baths. Here decorations give the environment a marine atmosphere with a green-azure pool and a vaulted ceiling with a painting of an aquarium filled with fish.

A door in the dressing room (across from the one we entered) leads to the *tepidarium* for warm water baths. The floor of this room was raised to create an air space where warm air circulated. The floor is decorated with a mosaic of *Triton surrounded by four dolphins* – in tone with the marine style found in the women's section of the baths, which is almost identical.

We move on to the fourth room: here we find the *caldarium* for hot water baths. A large bathing tub is still visible and on the back wall, we find a labrum (similarly to the

THE WOMEN'S SECTION OF THE BATHS

(See guide page 22; map ❾)

One enters a large room with a square shape surrounded by a bench, which served as a waiting area. As was usual for the times, the women's baths were smaller and less elegant than the men's baths and they did not always exist in all towns. However, in this case, though it was smaller, it has reached us in a much greater state of conservation.

The current entrance is not the original one, which was actually at n. 9, preceded by a small portico. The changing room or apodyterium, in good condition, features a barrel vault with stucco fluting, a black and white mosaic floor depicting Triton with dolphins, octopus and morays and large shelves used for clothing. Similar features are found in the tepidarium, where the pavement is decorated with a strip in geometric design, while the large calidarium is easily recognizable by its double-layer flooring, visible through an opening protected by a grate, through which hot air circulated.

In addition to the large tub for soaking, the space has a circular foundation intended to support the labrum for ablutions and two fine marble seats, one in white marble and the other in antique red.

The Women's Section of the Baths, as it was and as it is. ➢
Above, Detail of a mosaic floor.

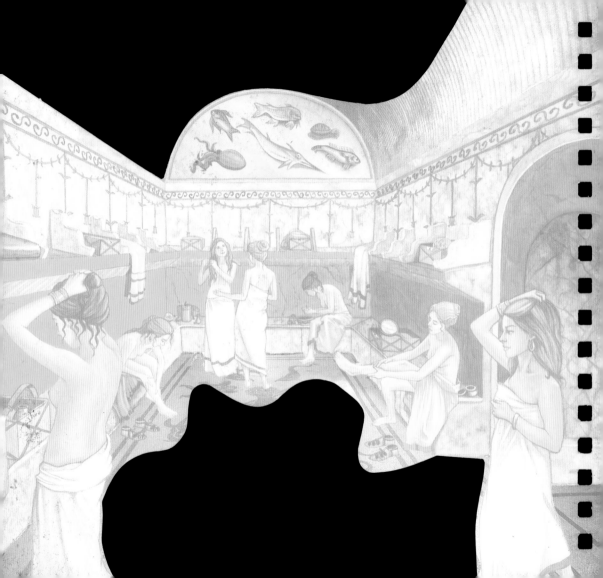

HOUSE OF THE OPUS CRATICIUM *(See guide page 22; map ⑫)*

This interesting construction technique was preserved thanks to the eruption of Herculaneum. By covering the city with lava instead of ash like Pompeii, it made the excavation more difficult but it maintained the organic materials such as wood and bamboo.

These two materials were woven together to make framework (opus craticium) which was then filled with pebbles and lime mortar. Aside from the fact that this was a cheaper way to build, the lightness of the construction made it suitable even if the ground was not well consolidated.

The downsides were that it was much less resistant to fire and to humidity. Inside, the construction is divided into two small apartments that are well separated.

A third apartment belongs to the shop, which displays a wooden hoist used to raise water from a well.

This is an example of a less expensive home, which was far from the traditional domus. No remains of this kind were found in Pompeii, which appears to have had a less varied urban design than Herculaneum.

House of the Opus Craticium as it is (right) and as it was (in front).

frigidarium) beneath the apse for washing with cold water.

Once again on *Cardo IV* (*number 8, see map* ❾), we find the entrance to the **women's section of the Baths**. It opens at the back of the same block as the men's baths (*see the information on page 16*).

The tour picks back up at the Decumanus Inferior. There are a number of shops on this road that were created from areas once belonging to the House of the Wooden Partition, which we see next to it.

The **Lanarius Shop** is especially interesting (*number 9, see map* ❿) as it contains an extremely rare example of a tool: a wooden screw press used to iron clothing.

Found in the hardened lava, it was adjusted, reassembled and placed behind a protective glass screen – it looks almost ready to be used. The next door leads to the **House of the Wooden Partition** (*insula III, n. 11, see map* ⓫ *and info p. 24*). Once again on Cardo IV, (*insula III, nos. 13-14 -15, see map* ⓬) we find a very interesting example of a multi-family building: the **House of the Opus Craticium** (*see info p. 20*).

We pick back up the tour along Cardo IV continuing towards the higher part of the city: a number of homes face the road.

Most of them are wealthier homes like the **House of the Mosaic Atrium** (*insula IV, nos. 1-2, see map* ⓭), named for the beautiful geometric white and black mosaic tesserae that welcome visitor's at the entrance.

The floor has sunk due to the ground giving way under the weight of the lava flow. It is another beautiful example of a panoramic house with a large Triclinium (dining room) facing the garden and portico.

Beyond that are a covered loggia and a *terrace with a sea view* making for a splendid panorama, which is probably the most characteristic aspect of the home.

On the long side of the garden, we find a beautiful slightly raised exedra decorated with

Above, entrance to the House of the Mosaic Atrium (floor).

mythological characters against a landscape (*the Punishment of Dirce and Diana bathing*). In front of the Baths we find the **Samnite House** (*insula V, n. 1, see map* ⑭) which was named for the fact that more than any other home in Herculaneum, it represents the characteristics of the last pre-Imperial era, the Samnite period, dating back to the end of the second century B.C.

Its Italianate structure is particularly evident in the lovely *Tuscan style atrium*, crowned by a gracious loggia with small columns connected by a railing.

The elegant entryway is framed by inset columns crowned with tuff stone Corinthian capitols. The atrium is decorated with Pompeii style frescoes, which were obviously added later. The *Tablinium* (office) has a lovely floor decorated with a large rosette of diamond shapes surrounding a small round copper tile. (*continues on page 28*)

The Samnite House.

THE HOUSE OF THE WOODEN PARTITION

(See guide page 22; map ⑪)

The façade of this building is especially interesting since it has been conserved almost completely intact all the way up to the second floor. This makes it possibly the most complete view of a private home in the imperial era still in existence. The door is a simple yet crowned by an elegant beaded cornice, which matches the windows on the upper floor. On this upper floor an independent entrance is used (n. 10 in the insula) which proves how many patrician homes were modified during the last years of Herculaneum due to the expansion of the wealthy merchant class whose desire was to live in the most aristocratic homes.

It owes its name to the wooden divider placed between the large atrium and the tablinum, decorated with bronze studs, which has come down to us virtually intact, although obviously charred. The excellent state of conservation of the building's white façade is striking; the large doorway stands out, framed by blocks of tuff, between small windows that remind us how, in Roman homes, light and air came mainly from the interior courtyards. Worthy of note is the large Tuscan-type atrium, mentioned earlier for the wooden partition that separates it from the tablinum; both are evidence of a rather archaic character, even though the pictorial decoration in Style IV dates to the final phase of Herculaneum's life.

Opening off the atrium are bedrooms (cubicola), in one of which was found the wooden bed, charred as usual. The tablinum, decorated with lovely frescoes on a red background, was the room of access to the garden, surrounded on three sides by a peristyle with columns and semicolumns, while the fourth side was closed off by a wall frescoed with garden views and topped by a scenic portico. Various rooms face the garden; to the right a passageway leads to the service area, where we find kitchen and latrine, side by side. The passageway communicates as well with the shop that faces the 3rd cardo, where two dolia can be seen: these are large jars used to keep foodstuffs.

Below, the Wooden Partition.　　　*The House of the Wooden Partition, as it was and as it is.* ➤

Ahead we find the entrance of the **House of the Carbonised Furniture** (*insula V, n.5, see map* **15**). It was named for the furniture (a small table and dining couch) which are still displayed where they were found.

The *Triclinium* is quite interesting with rich decorative paintings in the fourth Pompeian style and a beautiful multi-hued marble floor. The elegant Tablinium is ornate with flying female figures on the wall and a sleeping area that has a picture of *Pan finding a sleeping nymph*. The temple-shaped Lararium (a shrine to the household deities) at the end of the courtyard has fine stucco decorations.

Next we reach the **House of Neptune and Amphitrite** (*insula V, n.7, see map* **16** *and info on page 30*). The splendid mosaic, which gives the house its name, is located in the lovely nymphaeum (water garden) at the end of the summer dining area, the Triclinium.

A carbonized piece of furniture found at the House of the Carbonized Furniture.

Another interesting home is the **House of the Beautiful Courtyard** (*insula V, n. 29, see map* **⑰**), which has a very unusual layout. Instead of the usual atrium and vestibule, we find a large rectangular room with a low ceiling lit by a window overlooking the road and by light from the internal courtyard that it connects to. This courtyard gave the house its name and it definitely is beautiful with a masonry staircase above a niche decorated in plant motifs with a shaped and painted parapet and balcony that is also adorned with elegant paintings. The *floor is a fine geometric mosaic.*

The staircase leads to the upper floor rooms connected organically with the ground floor marking the passage from the more archaic atrium-styled homes, which were typically single-family dwellings with only one floor, to homes with courtyards where the ground floor and first floor were clearly subdivided. (*continues on page 34*)

The House of the beautiful Courtyard - detail of the interior.

HOUSE OF NEPTUNE AND AMPHITRITE

(See guide page 28; map **16**)

The atrium has a classic impluvium and Lararium decorated with a small statue of Jupiter and a small bronze herma sculpture of Hercules. A tablinium at the end with coloured marble flooring and walls decorated in the fourth style have unfortunately deteriorated. The room opens towards the most enjoyable part of the home, the triclinium. Here the lack of a garden is made up for with illusionistic trompe l'oeil painting which simulates a pergola on the eastern wall, which was most likely similar to the area it covered originally.

Among other elegant mosaics on the walls are Neptune and Amphitrite framed in an elaborate architectural composition made with glass paste mosaics and shell borders. The fountain located at the centre of the triclinium was fed by a larger fountain that served as the water tank. It was located behind the triclinium inside a nymphaeum that was also decorated in rich mosaics with coloured plant motifs on a blue background, with peacocks and with a deer being chased by dogs.

The rooms on the upper floor, which can even be seen from the road, were built later because the earthquake that preceded the eruption destroyed part of the design. It was probably during that restoration that the **shop** was built next to the entrance (insula V, n. 6). It is one of the best preserved in Herculaneum and it connected with the rest of the building and belonged to the rich owner. Furnished with care, it has reached us in almost a perfect state with fava beans and chick peas still on the counter for sale and amphorae for wine stacked neatly on the shelves - all abandoned as they tried to escape to safety.

Above and on the right: detail of the mosaic.   *House of Neptune and Amphitrite, as it was and as it is.* ➢

In front of the last house we find the **House of the Black Hall** (*insula VI, n. 13, see map* ⓲) named for the paintings in the large hall located at the end of the peristyle. At the entrance of the home, the carbonised remains of the doorposts and lintel are still intact. The entrance leads to the *atrium* with a marble-lined impluvium, an elegant portico surrounded by columns with flooring made from ground brick and mortar with coloured marble inserts. On the sides, we find the *cubiculum* (small rooms frequently used for sleeping or private meetings) the *kitchen* and the *tablinium* which also has a floor made from ground brick mortar, one of the largest in Herculaneum built in *opus incertum* style. The walls are decorated in the fourth style with a lower and upper border in red panels developed around an *aedicule* at the centre crowned by a tympanum, with architectural views at the ends of the walls. Continue through the *peristyle* and on the right there is a large hall (7.8 x 5.3 meters) for which the house

The House of the Black Hall.

is named that contains frescoes on a black background in fourth style, which is typically very refined, next to a formal hall and living area, which is also decorated, with frescoes.

We continue along Cardo IV, which soon leads to the **Decumanus Maximus** *(see map* ⑲*)*. The intersection is marked by a *public fountain* with rather unrefined relief work. It portrays *Venus bathing* and a *mask of Gorgon*. This point may be considered as the city centre.

From here, the townspeople could access the Forum, which was the seat of political, religious and commercial life in the city, as well as a number of public buildings. Only a few of these have been excavated in recent years such as the large building with the portico facing several shops, which served as the **mercantile Forum**. Next to this was a large

four-sided Arch *(see map* ⑳*)* covered in marble and white stucco figures and finely worked rosettes next to four honorary statues that marked the division between the market Forum and the **civil Forum**. The Basilica is still the most important public building to have been uncovered. In front of it we find **College of the Augustali** *(insula VI, n. 21, see map* ㉑ *and information on p. 38)*.

If we return to the southern side of the Forum (across Cardo IV nos. 15-16 of insula V) we reach the famous **House of the Bicentenary** *(insula V, n. 15, see map* ㉒*)*, named for the bicentennial celebrations taking place the year it was discovered in commemoration of the beginning of the excavation of Herculaneum. The lower floor rooms are quite elegant in-

(continues on page 40)

35

The four-sided Arch (above). The House of the Bicentenary (below).

COLLEGE OF THE AUGUSTALI

(See guide page 35; map **㉑***)*

Inscription dedicated to Augustus.

The College of the Augustali was a religious centre for the worship of Augustus. Most of the members were liberti (freed men) who became Augustali in order to mainstream into the city's social life. The large quadrangular building has delicate walls with enclosed arches and central columns. On the left wall we see the entrance of Hercules in Olympus accompanied by Jupiter, Juno and Minerva. On the right, the fresco shows Hercules fighting Achelous. At the back, was the porter's room, built in opus craticium - the porter's skeleton was found on the bed. An inscription on the wall states that the building was dedicated to Augustus (27 BC – 14 AD) who was living at the time, and that it was built by brothers A. Lucius Proculus and A. Lucius Iulianus, who offered lunch to the members of the municipal senate and the Augustali on the day it was inaugurated. The side entrance to this unusual and interesting structure, one of the few in Herculaneum that can be defined in some way as public, is found at the outer wall in opus reticulatum and brick, at n. 24. Some graffiti inside attributes the name of Curia Augustana to this building. This appears to be underscored by the fact that statues representing Caesar and Augustus, today lost, were placed on the two bases, still present, alongside the columns flanking the entrance. The interior appears as a vast, rectangular hall, in the center of which stand four columns set at the corners of a quadrangular opening, supported by an entablature consisting of large wooden beams, obviously charred. The two rear columns were encompassed in two partitions which, resting on the rear side of the hall, formed a small quadrangular space with a base intended to hold the statue of Augustus, as is clearly indicated by the laurel crown painted on the wall, the typical Imperial civic crown. The walls are decorated with Style IV frescoes, with two central scenes devoted to the mythological hero who gave his name to Herculaneum, depicting the Introduction of Hercules to Olympus and Hercules' Struggle with the River Acheloos.

Painting depicting Hercules (below).   *College of the Augustali, as it was and as it is.* ➤

College of the Augustali.

The House of the Corinthian Atrium.

cluding the large *atrium* with lovely *mosaic flooring* and the refined Tablinium (office) with painted decorations and a *folding wooden gate*, which is partially original. A very interesting discovery was made on the upper floor: for decades, it was considered the most important find at the home – a cross-shaped emblem on a wall inside a stucco panel. Many archaeologists including Amedeo Maiuri and Margherita Guarducci thought it had religious significance as the oldest known reference to the cross before 79 AD. Recent theories suggest that the wall marking might have been left by the imprint of a bracket that once hung on the wall. The Decumanus Maximus leads to Cardo V and on the right we find the **House of the Corinthian Atrium** (*insula V n. 30, see map* ㉓) which is small yet refined. The *atrium* is decorated with six Corinthian columns covered in white and red stucco from which the house takes its name. Instead of an impluvium pool to catch rainwater, we find a gracious fountain adorned with plants and flowers. After the construction of the city aqueducts, the original purpose of the impluvium became redundant. Next door we find the **House of the Wooden Sacellum** (*insula V, n. 31, see map* ㉔) named after an unusual dual-purpose furnishing. Found in an alcove to the right of the entrance, it is a small *cabinet-Lararium*. Shaped like a temple, it had split doors flanked by two

Bronze fountain portraying the Lernaean Hydra.

fluted Corinthian columns, which contained statuettes of the household gods (*Lari*). The lower section was a simple cabinet used to contain glass and terracotta dishes. The entrance to the **Palestra** (gym) is on the opposite side of Cardo V (*Insula Orientalis II, n. 4, see map* ㉕). It covers around 110 x 80 meters in the eastern part of Herculaneum under the viaduct at the entrance. The gigantic complex was built in the Augustan era (27 BC – 14 AD) and it is still being excavated and restored. The main en-

trance is a grandiose *vestibule* flanked by two columns. From there we reach a large open area surrounded by a portico on three sides and a cryptoporticus (a covered portico) crowned by a panoramic terrace above. There are a number of rooms along the western side of the portico. One of the most interesting is a *large rectangular apsidal room* that is almost 10 meters in height with a niche at the back and a large central white and grey marble table used for displaying the prizes to be awarded to competition champions. At the centre is a *large cruciform pool*, which has *bronze fountain* portraying the *Hydra of Lerna*, the mythical five-headed serpent, wound around a tree trunk. (*continues on page 46*)

41

The open Palestra.
Rectangular apsidal room of the Palestra, above.

THE HOUSE OF THE RELIEF OF TELEPHUS

(See guide page 46; map **27** *)*

The large and ample House of the Relief of Telephus was built with an interesting layout in order to resolve a number of problems: the ground was not level and the formal rooms needed to face the south of the city in order to enjoy the splendid view of the sea. It also had to be built around the adjacent pre-existing House of the Gem. After passing through an airy vestibule, we enter the atrium, which has an original almost Greek style form: it is divided into three naves divided by two lines of columns. The spaces between the columns were decorated with "oscilla" which were very finely sculpted marble relief disks of theatre masks and satyrs. A cabinet displays some of the interesting domestic items found – a necklace of amulets and food. The red columns and walls enhance the suggestive atmosphere.

The area beneath the house, which faces another direction, is connected to the atrium by a ramp that leads to the peristyle and by an internal hallway that is quite steep (located next to the tablinium). This leads to the large peristyle with brick columns that enclose the spacious garden with a rectangular pool at the centre. Three drawing rooms with rich marble decorations face the garden. Through another hallway, we reach a panoramic terrace facing the south with other rooms opening off of it. One of the rooms has incredible marble decorations that are truly fit for an emperor. In a small room near this one, we find the relief representing "the legend of Telephus" (or Orestes) which gave the house its name.

The Relief of Telephus. *The House of the Relief of Telephus, as it was and as it is.* ➢

On the opposite side of Cardo V, on the corner of the Decumanus Inferior we find the **Large Tavern** or **Thermopolium** (*insula IV, n. 12, see map* ㉖ *and info p. 48*), a small building with an atrium and two rooms with frescoes in the *fourth style*, which are still partially intact.

Continuing on Cardo V, which winds down the hill of Herculaneum to the bastions that mark the end of the city, stop and look at the **House of the Relief of Telephus** (*insula I, nos. 2-3, see map* ㉗ *and info p. 42*).

We have already mentioned the **House of the Gem** (*insula I, n. 1, see map* ㉘), which takes its name from a small piece of jewellery with an engraved portrait of a woman which dates back to the era of Claudius I (1st century AD). The atrium entrance has beautiful black and red decorations.

After passing through a hall and a vestibule with a white and black mosaic floor, we reach a large hall that faces the terraces as do the surrounding large and luminous rooms.

Like all of the homes that face the steep southern slope of Herculaneum (justly described as panoramic homes), this house was designed around the view so that the formal living areas would face the sea.

We will continue down Cardo V: the road descends at this point and becomes more enclosed until reaching the tunnel of Porta Marina. Here we find the most beautiful home in

The House of the Gem.

the southern section of Herculaneum: The **House of the Deer** (*insula IV, n. 21, see map* 29 *and information p. 54*), which stands out for its beautiful location and can clearly be seen by anyone who stops to look at the excavations in the square at the end of the entrance viaduct. The richness and elegance of the rooms has been highlighted by the major restoration works carried out at the turn of the millennium to restore the frescoes and the building rooftops

The House of the Deer.

THE LARGE TAVERN *(See guide page 46; map ㉖)*

The Thermopolium was the largest shop found during the excavations. Here they sold hot and cold drinks much like cafes today. There are still eight (dolia) vases, which were used to hold the grains, beans and drinks that sat in an L-shaped marble counter. One of the amphoras has a painted inscription by a Herculaneum manufacturer M. Livi Alcini Herculani.

At the end of the counter small marble shelves were used to set the dirty dishes. There was another larger dolium on the floor while the south-eastern corner most likely held a latrine due to the type of flooring.

Other connected rooms were used for storage and there was also a dining room where customers could eat and drink. On a wall of the partition, graffiti that may have been written by a customer says in Greek, "Diogenes the cynic, in seeing a woman swept away by a river, exclaimed: Let one ill be carried away by another".

The Large Tavern (Thermopolium).　　　*The Large Tavern, as it was and as it is.* ➤

THE SACRED AREA AND THE SUBURBAN BATHS

The southern edge of Cardo V is marked by the city walls, which were built over a number of imperial eras, as well as luxurious private homes with panoramic waterfront views and two important public complexes related to religion and services.

At the centre is a large **terrace** *(see map ③⓪)* that is raised slightly above sea level, to make room for the so-called "fornici" which were used as boathouses and will be discussed more thoroughly later. Face the sea and look right over the **Sacred Area** *(see map ③②)* – a fenced area enclosing the *Temple of Venus* and the *Temple of the four divinities (Minerva, Vulcan, Mercury and Neptune)* which is larger and has more sophisticated marble work than the

52

The Sacred Area (on the left). Terrace of M. Nonio Balbo (on the right).

first. The open-air sacrificial areas are in front of each of the temples. Next to the entrance to these areas are two small rooms: the first contained two frescoes of mythological scenes and the second contained two headless female statues with togas and a *marble altar* dedicated to Venus.

On the opposite side of the terrace we find a small plaza with a *marble altar* at the centre bearing a long inscription (on the side facing the sea) of the honorary decree issued by the municipal senate in honour of *M. Nonio Balbo*. The **statue** of this important patron of the city during the Augustan era was recently restored and placed in the square, which contains the Suburban Baths (*see map* ㉛ *and information p. 60*).

Statue of M. Nonio Balbo.

The Sacellum of the four gods: shrine to Vulcan, Neptune, Mercury and Minerva.

THE HOUSE OF THE DEER (See guide page 47; map **29**)

The House of the Deer was named for a sculpture that decorated the garden, but it most likely belonged to Q. Granius Verus, who was a member of one of Herculaneum's most prominent families. The entrance (one the northern side) opens onto a small atrium and balcony. The service and kitchen area is on the right and a large cryptoporticus and garden are on the left. The small white mosaic tesserae on the floor of the entryway are interspersed with larger pieces of coloured marble with a black border. The window-lined walls of the cryptoporticus are decorated with fourth style frescoes portraying Cupids, still life themes and sea views, though many of the originals have been moved to the National Archaeological Museum in Naples.

The central garden area contained a number of statues including the deer statue for which he house was named. Many of the original statues have been transferred to the museum in Naples and replaced by copies.

The Triclinium is located on the northern side with plain black fresco panels framed in red to adorn the walls and fine marble on the floor. Next to it, we find another room with red walls and a red ceiling, which contains a head of Minerva at the centre and a large bronze bathtub.

To the south of the garden in the panoramic part of the home, the lovely summer Triclinium is completed by a portico with a splendid view of the sea and a pergola supported by four columns and the original flower pots.

54

The House of the Deer, as it was and as it is. ➤

The boat pavilion and the beachfront "fornici".

Near the *suburban baths* in 1983, a discovery was made which eloquently sums up the tragic story of Herculaneum. Researchers discovered a large 9-meter boat with a maximum width of 2.2 meters and a maximum height of around 1 meter from the keel to the edge, which seems to be carbonised and crushed at the centre, though it is extraordinarily well preserved. The boat is kept in a special

pavilion at the *excavation Museum* and a fibreglass coating inside a steel structure protects it.
The most interesting discovery over the course of the excavations during those years was the discovery of the **"fornici"** (*see map* ㉝) on the beach. At the time of the eruption, the sea was 300 meters further back than it is currently. There are *twelve rooms with vaulted ceilings* that in all probability were used as boathouses. *270 bodies* were found inside: victims of Herculaneum trying desperately to escape disaster. Each boathouse contained dozens of persons gathered at the back in an effort to save themselves.

VILLA OF THE PAPYRI

Located to the west of the urban centre almost 300 meters from the archaeological area, we find the splendid **Villa dei Papyri**, which can be reached directly through a tunnel connecting the ancient beach with the current entrance, which is still under construction. The tunnel will pass beneath the houses of ancient Herculaneum and thanks to the use of super modern multimedia equipment, visitors will be able to physically immerse themselves in history and relive the effects of the 79 AD eruption.
The villa is located around 25 meters below the surface with a large front over 250 meters long. Knowledge of its existence has been around since the first excavation of Herculaneum and it was explored between 1762 and 1764 with the standard tunnel system. It turned out to be of exceptional importance. Beautiful sculptures (58 bronze and 21 marble sculptures) created a truly splendid collection that was clearly inspired on the philosophical and cultural ideas of the owner.

The "Fornici" boathouses.

Transferred to the Royal Palace of Portici Museum, they were later transferred the National Archaeological Museum in Naples. The *papyrus* documents found there are kept at the National Library. The manuscripts are priceless and they gave Swiss researcher Karl Jacob Weber the name for the villa, whose owner was identified as Lucius Calpurnius Piso Caesoninus (Caesar's father-in-law and console in 58 BC) though there are also other hypotheses. 1826 carbonised papyrus scrolls were found containing mostly Greek works of Epicurean philosophy. Many attempts have been made to read them since they were discovered. Piarist father Antonio Piaggio invented a "traction machine" that was used to unroll the material and it remained in use up to the beginning of the nineteen hundreds.

Over the course of the twentieth century, technologies that are more sophisticated have been used to read the carbonized scrolls. In 1988 Professor Marcello Gigante, a philologist and papyrologist working with Brigham Young University, developed a new digital photographic technique created by NASA at the Officina dei Papiri Ercolanensi (at the National Library in Naples) which is today dedicated to the eminent scholar. Recent excavations, which began anew after two centuries, have made it possible to comprehend the height of the grand complex with four storeys along the slope, which can be excavated in the future.

In the traditional plan of the complex, there are five fundamental centres; the *atrium quarter*, which is the only one that has been fully excavated.

The library zone, where the famous rolls of papyrus were found, the *square peristyle*, which opens onto a large exedra; the large *rectangular peristyle* with the long sides measuring around 100 meters; the round *garden* with the panoramic view. Recent restoration works have been concentrated on the sixteen rooms on the main floor, with halls for receiving guests and holding banquets.

They are not all open to the public due to the fact that the humidity must be kept at a constant level to protect the exceptional wall frescoes and the stucco ceiling decorations in the second Pompeian style (I BC) as well as the mosaics which belonged to the era the villa was built (between 40 and 30 BC).

The bronze Runners.

THE SUBURBAN BATHS *(See guide page 52; map ③①)*

The large complex was mostly likely built by the eminent figure portrayed in the honorary statue. Built next to the buttresses of the House of the Gem and the House of the Relief of Telephus (which we have already visited), it is very well preserved because it is one of the few buildings with a roof still intact. It was also very difficult to reach, which discouraged early researchers who did not always use the best excavation methods. One enters on the original wooden staircase that leads to the vestibule, which is lit by a large open oculus in the ceiling.

The rooms are organised by warmth, which was customary in Roman Baths. The first room is the frigidarium, lit through a skylight in the vaulted ceiling. It contains a large tub covered in crushed brick mortar and fourth style wall decorations. The tepidarium follows with fine white stucco walls with seven mythological heroes depicted at the centre, which seem to underscore that these were the 'men's' baths, and a couple of cupids in white stucco relief.

The wood framing is original and worthy of note. The last room is the caldarium with flooring and floorboards in marble. The stucco wall decorations with imaginary themes were common in fourth style works.

Tetrastyle Atrium with a herma-style statue of Apollo. Caldarium, as it was and as it is. ➤

OPLONTIS - THE VILLA OF POPPEA

The suburban district of Pompeii named **Oplontis** (which lies under current day Torre Annunziata) was discovered in 1831. The district was destined to serve as the residence of the richest families and it was part of Pompeii. Here during excavations carried out in the 1960s a Roman villa was discovered that most likely belonged to Poppea Sabina (Nero's second wife).

The **Villa of Poppea** was buried (like Pompeii and Herculaneum) by the eruption of Vesuvius in 79 AD and it was discovered during excavations that took place between 1964 and 1984. The construction of the Villa began in the first century BC. At the time of the eruption, the villa was most likely being restored due to damage caused by the earthquake in 62 AD. As can be seen from the discovery of building and ornamental materials stored there ready to be installed and the lack of things belonging to daily life, the villa was uninhabited at the time of the eruption.

The Villa of Poppea.

The hypothesis that the villa belonged to Poppea comes from the discovery of an amphora with an inscription *"Secundo Poppaeae"* (to Secondo, servant of Poppea). After Poppea's death in 68 AD the villa passed to a new owner who in all likelihood began the restoration works, which were brusquely interrupted by the eruption of Mt. Vesuvius.

The villa contains over 90 rooms with formal halls, baths, cubicula and gardens. Many of the rooms still contain well-preserved splendid Pompeian frescoes.

It is formed by an older central nucleus that dates back to the first century BC, which faces north and south and is built around the atrium with decorations primarily in the Pompeian Second Style. Two other distinct sections are oriented to the west (containing the owner's quarters) and the east (with the servant's quarters and the production areas connected by a long hallway). The eastern section ends with a *large pool* and a large garden to the north of it (*Viridarium*), and with a smaller garden surrounded by a portico with columns (*peristyle*) to the south. In this area, which was newer, fourth style decorations dominate.

Most likely, at the beginning, one would have entered the villa

Triclinium frescoes with a decorative flair.

through a Tuscan atrium with an *impluvium* (a rectangular pool at the centre of the floor used to catch rainwater).

The atrium contained a *white mosaic floor* and walls decorated with second style frescoes depicting a faux colonnade at the sides of two doors, which have a figure of a *winged Victory* on each side. Two shields and medallions are painted above (in between) the columns with religious symbols in the lower area. To the right and to the left of the atrium we find

rooms richly decorated with masks and still life paintings with trompe l'oeil porticoes, gardens and backgrounds.

Villa di Poppea is a splendid example of a grandiose villa for leisure and pleasure: 130 meters long, 110 meters wide – it has a surface area of 3650 square meters (without taking into consideration the internal pergolas, pools and gardens).

The architectural principles used both in the design of the overall composition of the construction as well as in the open natural areas make the structure one of the most important of Imperial times that has reached us today.

The Villa of Poppea (Calidarium).

Delphic tripod, detail of the sanctuary of Apollo.

MOUNT VESUVIUS

Mount **Vesuvius** is an active explosive volcano that is currently dormant. It is located in the Campania region inside Mt. Vesuvius National Park, which was established in 1996. It is part of the Somma/Vesuvius mountain chain, it is 1281 meters high and it contains a crater that measures 500 meters in diameter. Located inside the coast of the Gulf of Naples, it is around 10 kilometres from the city and it is the first volcano to have been studied systematically. An unmistakeable icon of the Naples landscape, Mt. Vesuvius has been dormant since 1944. It erupted during March of that year and the echoes were mistaken for the rumbling bombs of World War II still raging in Europe and the world. However, since that time one of the most famous volcanoes on earth seems to have become silent. Some scientists claim that it is extinct. However, esteemed volcanologists have been keeping a diary of the volcano's activity over the centuries and that has brought to light an almost cadenced regularity between its dormant and active phases.

Depiction of the eruption of Mt. Vesuvius (79 AD).

Historical Information

Mount Vesuvius as we know it today, developed in a recent era – during the famous eruption of 79 AD when lava, ash, pumice and molten rock erupted from its progenitor Mount Somma and tragically submersed the cities of Herculaneum and Pompeii.

It is believed that 400,000 years ago, the zone of Vesuvius was subject to volcanic activity, but the mountain actually began to develop around 25,000 years ago, most likely as a volcano under the sea in the Gulf of Naples. It later emerged from the water to form an island and then grew to meet the mainland due to the accumulation of erupted materials. Between 19,000 years ago and 79 AD, periods of violent eruptions were interspersed by periods of dormancy.

However, Mt. Vesuvius did not always seem like an active volcano. For many centuries, it was a quiet mountain covered with gardens and vineyards except for the arid mountaintop. The incredible fertility of the surrounding land favoured the development of the Osci and Samnite settlements: Stabia, Pompeii and Herculaneum, which were unaware of the risks in the area.

Scientists more precisely refer to the mountain that is universally known as Mt. Vesuvius as Somma-Vesuvius. Originally, only Mt. Somma existed, but after several volcanic transformations and the eruption mentioned above, the tip of the mountain partially collapsed creating a large crater-like "caldera" which contains the large cone of Mt. Vesuvius making it a stratovolcano.

Aerial view of Vesuvius' central crater.

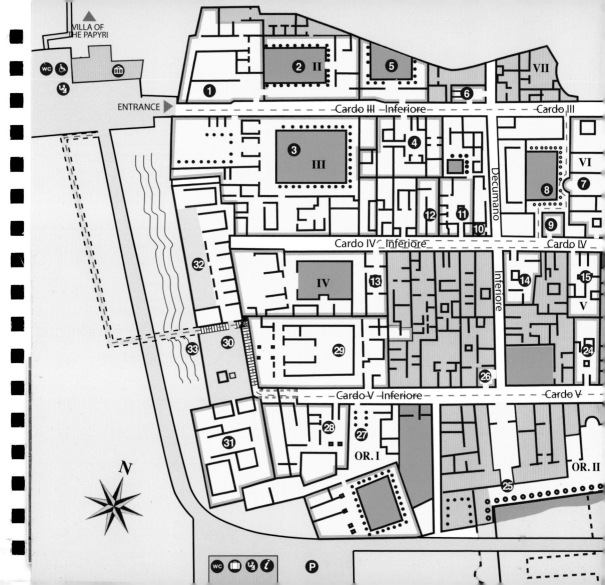

VILLA OF THE PAPYRI

wc ♿ ♻

🏛

ENTRANCE ►

Cardo III Inferiore — Cardo III

1
2 II
5
6
VII

3 III
4
8
VI
7
9
12
11
10
Decumano

Cardo IV Inferiore — Cardo IV

32
IV
13
14
15
V
Inferiore
24

33
30
29
26

Cardo V Inferiore — Cardo V

31
28
27
OR. I
25
OR. II

N

wc 🧳 ♻ ℹ

P

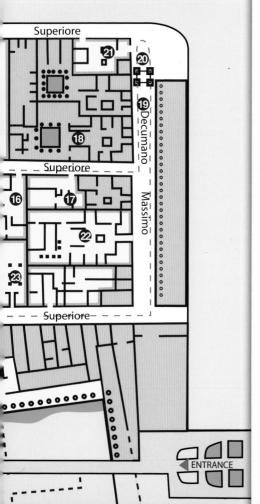